Pebble® Plus

Cats, Cats, Cats

Cat Behaviour

by Christina Mia Gardeski

raintree
a Capstone company — publishers for children

Raintree is an imprint of Capstone Global Library Limited, a company incorporated in England and Wales having its registered office at 264 Banbury Road, Oxford, OX2 7DY – Registered company number: 6695582

www.raintree.co.uk
myorders@raintree.co.uk

ISBN 978 1 4747 2260 5
20 19 18 17 16
10 9 8 7 6 5 4 3 2 1

British Library Cataloguing in Publication Data
A full catalogue record for this book is available from the British Library.

Editorial Credits
Jaclyn Jaycox, editor; Philippa Jenkins, designer;
Pam Mitsakos, media researcher; Steve Walker, production specialist

Photo Credits
Alamy: Juniors Bildarchiv GmbH, 9; Getty Images: Hill Street Studio, 19; Shutterstock: Diana Taliun, 21, Dmitri Ma, 7, Grey Carnation, 13, kmsh, 1, 17, Koldunov Alexey, cover, Oksana Kuzmina, 3, back cover, red rose, design element throughout, S. Castelli, 5, Sunny_baby, 11, The Len, 15

Printed and bound in China.

Contents

Why do cats do that?

Cats hide in boxes and rub against your legs. Have you ever wondered why they do these things and more? Let's find out!

A cat's miaow

Kittens miaow to tell their mothers they are hungry or scared. But adult cats miaow to tell people what they want. Most adult cats do not miaow at other cats.

Marked by a cat

Cats rub their bodies on people. This feels like a snuggle, but it is a mark. Cats leave their scent on the person. This tells other cats that the person is their owner.

Kitty kisses

Your cat stares at you with its eyes
half open. Then it blinks slowly.
Blink back! Some people think this
is a cat's way of giving you a kiss.

Kneading paws

Your cat starts to knead your lap.

It pushes its paws up and down.

Kittens do this to get milk from their

mother. Adult cats often knead when

they are happy.

Telling tails

Watch a cat's tail to see how the cat feels. Happy cats hold their tails high. The tail fur is flat. A cat that flicks its tail back and forth quickly is upset. Step back!

Cat-in-a-box

Cats like to fit themselves into shoe boxes, suitcases and other small spaces. They then watch what is happening around them. Small spaces make cats feel safe.

A cat's purr

Most cats purr when they are happy.

But some cats purr when they are

sick, hurt or afraid. Newborn kittens

cannot see or hear. Their mother

purrs so that they can find her.

On the hunt

Today most pet cats don't need to hunt for food. But they still pretend to hunt. They may hunt and follow a person's feet. Then they pounce!

21

Glossary

flick   make a quick movement

knead   push up and down with the paws

miaow   call or cry made by a cat

newborn   just born

pounce   jump on something suddenly and grab it

purr   make a low soft sound; animals such as cats purr

scent   smell of a person or thing

Read more

First Book of Cats, Isabel Thomas (A&C Black Childrens & Educational, 2014)

Kitty's Guide to Caring for Your Cat (Pets' Guides), Anita Ganeri (Raintree, 2013)

Looking after Cats and Kittens, Katherine Starke (Usborne Publishing Ltd, 2013)

Websites

www.cats.org.uk/cats-for-kids

Discover even more about cats! Read articles, watch videos and play games to learn all about cats and how to care for them.

www.rspca.org.uk/adviceandwelfare/pets/cats

Find out more about cat behaviour.

Comprehension questions

- Cats knead by pushing their paws up and down. Why do they knead?

- What does it mean when a cat is flicking its tail back and forth quickly?

- Cats purr for many different reasons. What is purring?

Index